Sabhya & Saachi Series

Authored and Conceptualized by:
Ms. Dimple Dang

Edited by:
Dr. Amit Dang

Illustrated and Designed by:
Mr. Tridib Ghosh (Team Chlorosynth)

Instagram: @sabhya.saachi

Note to parents

Dear Parents,

Thank you for choosing **"From Diapers To Undies - A Potty Training Tale"** for your child. We hope that this book will help make the potty training process a little easier and a lot more fun for your family.

Potty training can be a challenging time for both children and parents, but it's an important milestone in your child's development. Here are a few tips to keep in mind as you read this book with your child:

Take it slow: Potty training is a process that takes time and patience. Don't rush your child or expect them to be fully trained overnight. Celebrate the small victories and don't get discouraged by setbacks.

Make it fun: Potty training doesn't have to be a chore. Find ways to make it fun for your child, whether it's through reward charts, silly songs, or special treats with no bribery.

Encourage independence: As much as possible, let your child take the lead in their potty training journey. Encourage them to use the potty on their own and celebrate their successes.

Be positive: Potty training can be frustrating at times, but try to stay positive and avoid getting angry or upset with your child. Praise them for their efforts and let them know how proud you are of them.

We hope that this book helps your child feel excited and empowered about potty training. Thank you for choosing "Sabhya-Saachi Series".

Sincerely,
Dimple Dang

Sabhya **Saachi**

Saachi and Sabhya are a brother-sister duo who love to explore, play, and learn together. Saachi is the older sibling and she's always ready for adventure with her boundless energy and clever wit. Sabhya is the younger one, growing up fast and enthusiastic about discovering new things. Together, they are two peas in a pod, a double dose of adventure, and twice the fun!

© Dimple Dang 2023

All rights reserved

All rights reserved by author. No part of this publication may be reproduced, stored in a retrieval system or transmitted in any form or by any means, electronic, mechanical, photocopying, recording or otherwise, without the prior permission of the author. Although every precaution has been taken to verify the accuracy of the information contained herein, the author and publisher assume no responsibility for any errors or omissions. No liability is assumed for damages that may result from the use of information contained within.

First Published in **June 2023**

ISBN: 978-93-93385-66-6

BLUEROSE PUBLISHERS
www.BlueRoseONE.com
info@bluerosepublishers.com
+91 8882 898 898

Authored and Conceptualized by:
Ms. Dimple Dang

Edited by:
Dr. Amit Dang

Illustrated and Designed by:
Mr. Tridib Ghosh (Team Chlorosynth)

Distributed by:
BlueRose, Amazon, Flipkart

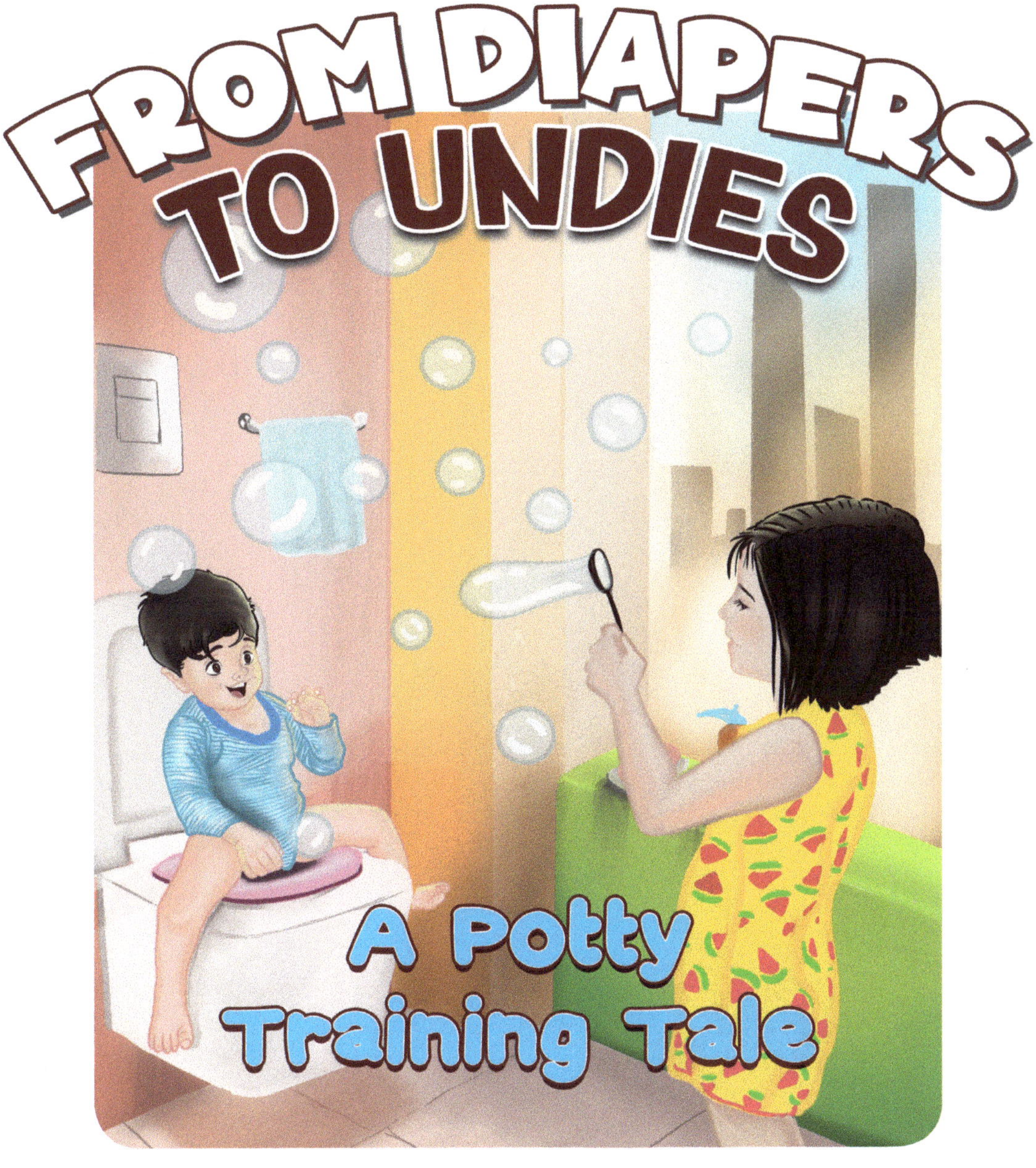

FROM DIAPERS TO UNDIES

A Potty Training Tale

Saachi: Hey what happened Sabhya? Why are you crying?

Sabhya: (crying) I don't like to wear a diaper, it gives me rashes. I want to wear big pants like you.

Saachi: Aww, you will get there soon Sabhya. Toilet training takes time and little practice.

Sabhya: (crying) But who is going to make me practice?

Saachi: Don't worry Sabhya! I'm there for you. I'm your best friend. Let me tell you a secret, I was just like you when I was your age.

Sabhya: (surprised) Really?

Saachi: Yes Sabhya! But look at me now, I am a big girl and can use the toilet all by myself.

Sabhya: I want to be big like you.

Saachi: Let us do this! Whenever you feel like "poo-poo", just sit back, relax and let it happen, while I blow bubbles for you. We will keep on trying this, till you make it happen.

Sabhya: Ok Saachi! I love you.

Sabhya: (excited) I did it, "poo-poo" is out! "poo-poo" done!
I pulled up my underpants too.

Saachi: (proud) See, I told you that you could do it. You are a big boy now.
I am flushing out toilet for you.

Saachi: Now it is time to wash your hands with soap and dry them with towel.

Sabhya: (curiously) Why I need to do that Saachi?

Saachi: This is to fight against germs like your favourite superhero.

Sabhya: (excited) Yay! I'm a superhero now.

Sabhya: (proud) Mumma Mumma!! I went to the toilet all by myself today.

Mother: (surprised) Oh is it? Look at you Sabhya. You are growing up so fast.

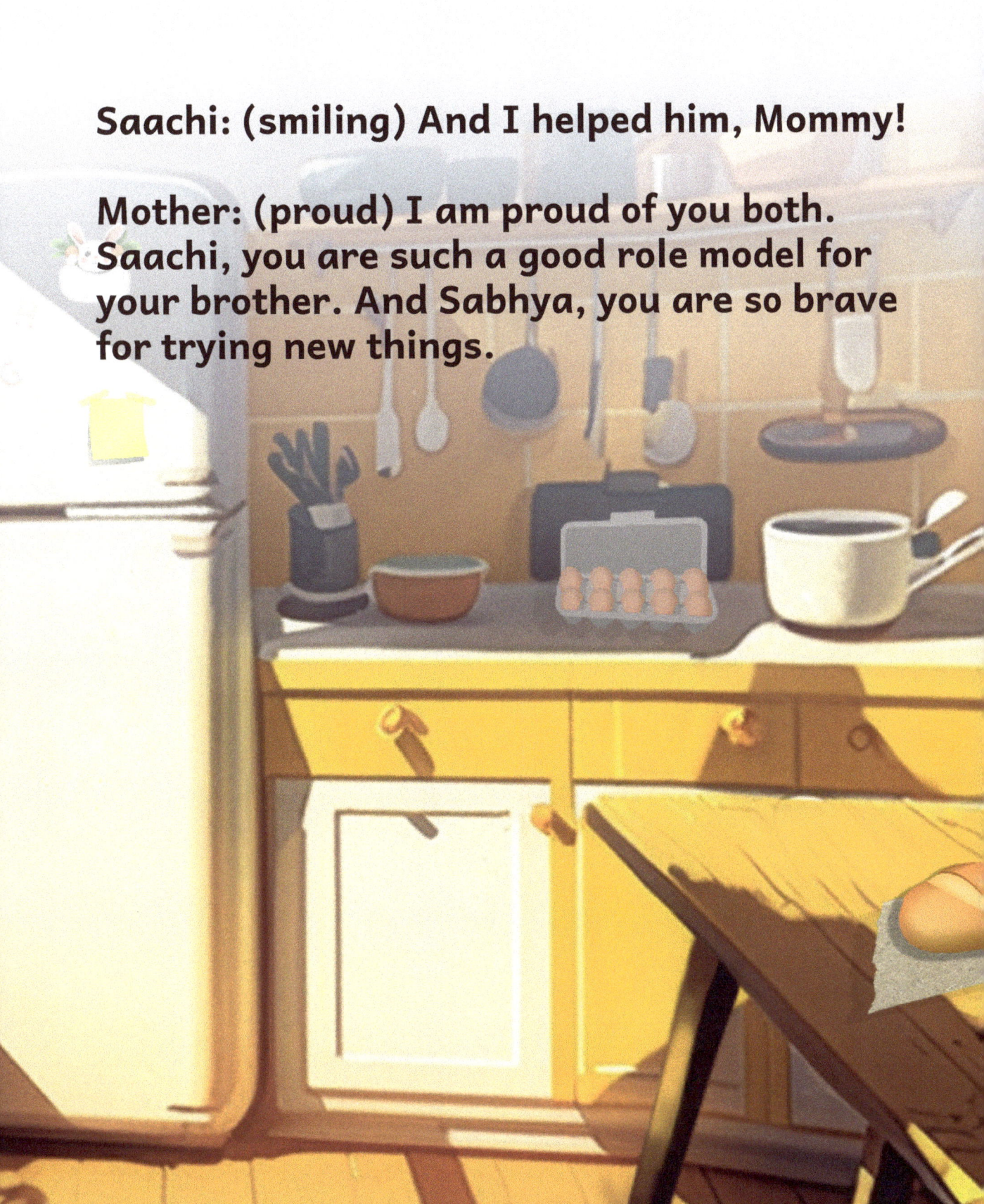

Saachi: (smiling) And I helped him, Mommy!

Mother: (proud) I am proud of you both. Saachi, you are such a good role model for your brother. And Sabhya, you are so brave for trying new things.

Saachi: (smiling) We make a great team, don't we Sabhya?

Sabhya: (smiling) Yeah, we do, my best friend!

Moral of the story

Patience and practice make a perfect combination to achieve whatever you want. And a helping hand from sibling or a friend can make the journey even more fun.

"Poo-Poo" training steps

Let's practice "poo-poo" training together with these 10 super simple steps....

1 Walk to the toilet and sit on your potty chair

5 Wash your "bum" with jet spray/water

6 Get down from the potty seat

7 Pull up your pants or put down your skirt

Washing Hands

- Hand Scrubbing
- Hand Cleaning
- Hand Washing
- Hand Rubbing
- Hand Hygiene
- Hand Sanitizing

Underpants

- Bloomer
- Boxer
- Shorts
- Pull-ups
- Knicker
- Underwear

www.ingramcontent.com/pod-product-compliance
Lightning Source LLC
LaVergne TN
LVHW070602070526
838199LV00011B/461